New Zealand's Remarkable Reforms

Fifth IEA Annual Hayek Memorial Lecture

Given in London on Tuesday, 4 June 1996

DONALD T BRASH
Governor, Reserve Bank of New Zealand

Occasional Paper 100

Published by
THE INSTITUTE OF ECONOMIC AFFAIRS
1996

First published in December 1996
by

THE INSTITUTE OF ECONOMIC AFFAIRS
2 Lord North Street, Westminster, London SW1P 3LB

Occasional Paper 100

ISSN 0073-909X
ISBN 0-255 36400-8

Printed in Great Britain by
HARTINGTON FINE ARTS LIMITED, LANCING, WEST SUSSEX

Set in Plantin 11 on 13 point

Contents

A Century of Occasional Papers

DR. DONALD BRASH'S PAPER, *New Zealand's Remarkable Reforms*, based on his 1996 Hayek Lecture, is the 100th Occasional Paper published by the Institute of Economic Affairs.

The IEA Occasional Paper series began in 1963 with George Stigler's *The Intellectual and the Market Place*. The purpose of the series was stated to be to publish '...essays and addresses not otherwise generally available in Britain'. Stigler's paper was a reprint of an address given to a college audience.

In the 33 years which have elapsed since that first Occasional Paper, some of the Institute's most influential papers have appeared in the series, some by economists who subsequently became Nobel Laureates. Many have been based on lectures – so making them available to a wider audience, as was the original intention of the series. Since 1970, for instance, the annual lecture given in honour of Harold Wincott has been published as an Occasional Paper.

To select just a few of the Papers, Harry Fern's *Towards an Independent University*, Occasional Paper No. 25 (1969), was the seminal work for the movement which founded the University of Buckingham; Axel Leijonhufvud's *Keynes and the Classics*, Occasional Paper No. 30 (1969) went to a Seventh Impression; Milton Friedman's immensely influential paper on monetary theory and policy, *The Counter Revolution in Monetary Theory*, given as Wincott Lecture No. 1, appeared as Occasional Paper No. 33 in 1970; Hayek's *Choice in Currency*, advocating freedom of choice among currencies, was Occasional Paper No. 48 in 1976.

Other authors of IEA *Occasional Papers* include such famous names in economics as James Buchanan, John Jewkes, Sir John Hicks, Sir Alan Peacock, James Meade, Lord Robbins, Graham Hutton, Sir Alan Walters, Roland Vaubel, Ben Roberts Arthur Seldon and Sir Samuel Brittan. Lord Harris's House of Lords speeches and his shorter articles have also appeared as *Occasional Papers*.

As the series goes beyond one hundred the Institute's range of lectures and similar events is widening: *Occasional Papers* will continue to disseminate the ideas expressed to a wide audience as well as providing a vehicle for shorter papers by IEA authors.

November 1996   COLIN ROBINSON
Editorial Director, Institute of Economic Affairs;
Professor of Economics, University of Surrey

Preface
by Geoffrey E. Wood*

NEW ZEALAND WAS FOR MANY YEARS A PROSPEROUS SOCIETY. Largely agricultural, it exported a substantial part of its output, mainly to the United Kingdom. The first shipment of frozen lamb from New Zealand to the UK left in April 1882, and by the 1890s the trade was booming. At the end of the 19th century, New Zealand (with, it should be said, a very small population) had one of the world's highest incomes per head. Some half century later, in the 1950s, when wool prices soared, New Zealand's income per head was again in the top 10 in the world.

A process of decline then set in, which did not start being reversed until the 1980s. In his fascinating Hayek Lecture, the fifth in that series, Dr Donald Brash, Governor of the Reserve Bank of New Zealand, examines the final years of decline and traces the course of recovery so far.

This Preface aims first to set out the most striking points of Dr Brash's account, and then to use that account, *first*, to suggest some general lessons for economic liberalisation and, *second,* to draw some lessons for economic policy in the United Kingdom.

The Background to Reform

An important aspect of reform in New Zealand is that not only have policies been changed, but the processes by which policy is determined have themselves undergone fundamental reforms. By making these processes more 'transparent' – a term often used in New Zealand policy-making – these reforms have been embedded, made hard to reverse, probably close to the maximum extent possible in any democracy which does not have a formal constitution.

---

* I am indebted to Paul Atkinson, Forrest Capie and David Henderson for discussions which greatly helped in preparing this preface.

What was there to be reformed? What was the background to these changes? In terms of the ratio of public expenditure to GNP there had been a rapid climb in the 10 years before 1984, the year when the reform process accelerated. The ratio climbed by 10 percentage points, to about 45 per cent – a peak for New Zealand since the end of the Second World War, but not as high as in some countries. In Belgium, Denmark, and Sweden, the ratio exceeded 60 per cent, and a few others had figures over 50 per cent.

Nor was New Zealand unique in the extent of detailed intervention in the economy – although, as Dr Brash points out, it contained some truly startling examples of such intervention, most notably perhaps that a doctor's prescription was required to allow the purchase of margarine. The New Zealand economy was among the most protectionist in the OECD area, and it was unique in that group in relying extensively on import licensing. Exchange controls over capital movements were restrictive – but no more so than those of France, Italy, and Scandinavia. Its labour markets were closely regulated, certainly in ways distinct from most other developed economies but perhaps no more rigidly than some. And since 1982, wages, prices, dividends, and interest rates had been controlled; but again, this was not unique, since similar controls could be found in several Southern European economies.

A fair summary would be that the New Zealand economy was not the most subject to government regulation of any country in the developed world, but it was indubitably among the leaders. What makes the New Zealand of these years stand out from the interventionist pack? It was characterised by a difference in attitude. In New Zealand (and also to a great extent in Australia) external economic policy was defensive; the economy was to be kept 'judiciously insulated from the rest of the world'.[1]

Donald Brash identifies several Hayekian themes in the response to this situation. First, and surely most important, there was '...a spectacular collapse of the mental defences against the intellectual counter-revolution which Hayek had begun in the 1940s...'(pp.19-20).

Second, and particularly affecting the policy-making process, 'the reforms reflected Hayek's view of the market-place as a

---

[1]   David Henderson, 'Economic Reform: New Zealand in an International Perspective', working draft, 1996.

"discovery procedure"'(p.20). This, Dr Brash argues, has led to great openness of economic policy-making in New Zealand, since with that view of the market it was important for there to be a free flow of information to the private sector, so as to let decision-making in that sector be as efficient as possible.

Reflecting Hayek's study of the institutional underpinnings of a free society, and his urging that the rule of law should comprise a 'uniform set of rules of conduct across society as a whole, without favouring or discriminating against any special interests' (pp.20-21), no sector of the economy received special treatment, favourable or unfavourable. What were the main changes these principles produced?

The Changes

There were changes affecting both the efficiency of resource allocation, that is to say, *micro-economic* changes; and changes affecting the total of output and the rate of inflation, *macro-economic* changes, which affect the environment in which micro-economic decisions are taken.

At the micro-economic level, the financial sector was liberalised, with all controls on credit, dividends, and so forth removed. (Wage and price controls were abolished at the same time.) The process continued with dramatic changes to banking supervision, made in January 1996; banks now have to make public much more information than previously, and supervision by the central bank is correspondingly lighter.

Foreign trade was also liberalised and, in 1991, labour market contracts made in their essentials no different from other commercial contracts. Contracts can be individual or collective, and employees can choose their own bargaining agents. There are still restrictions which affect the labour market but not other markets – the labour market still gets some degree of special treatment. But the effects of the changes there are nonetheless impressive. Of those Dr Brash lists undoubtedly the most notable is that rapidly accelerating productivity growth has

'...not been achieved at the expense of employment: on the contrary...unemployment has fallen rapidly over the last few years, while numbers employed have increased at an average of some 3·3 per cent per annum since 1991'(p.27).

Still at the micro-economic level, there was reform of the structure of taxation. A broad-based sales tax was introduced; the only exemption was for financial services. This both reduced distortions and reduced compliance and collection costs. (There is a lesson here for the UK.) Income-tax rates were cut, and the number of rates was itself reduced. At the same time the tax base was broadened. The changes, Dr Brash notes, led the OECD to observe that the New Zealand tax system was probably the least distorting in the OECD. There were reforms, all of which Dr Brash discusses, in housing, education and (particularly notable) health care, where there has been separation of purchaser and provider and increased use of charging.

At the same time, assistance to the poor was not abolished but supplied increasingly in the form of cash, thus allowing them to make their own decisions about their spending priorities. The belief apparently held by many welfare bureaucracies, that to be poor is to be too stupid to make decisions, has not spread to New Zealand.

There were reforms to the public sector, designed to make it more efficient. Departments manage their own finances, guided by a 'Chief Executive' who contracts with government ministers for the supply of services. These contracts, in line with the desire for openness, are tabled in Parliament. The Reserve Bank was also given its own, somewhat similar, contract, again characterised by transparency in objective together with great freedom in how to achieve the objective. Dr Brash, not surprisingly, discusses that contract in some detail (pp.33-34 and 41-43). The public sector moved to accruals accounting; taking in amounts due but unpaid, amounts owed, and, very important, unfunded pensions liabilities.

Privatisation was extensive. The noteworthy feature here is the attitude to competition. Rather than create a special regulatory framework, firms were privatised only when they were entering markets judged to be competitive. (Whether this judgement was always well founded is a matter for dispute.)

At the macro-economic level, both fiscal and monetary policy were changed radically, both in what they tried to do and in how they went about doing it. On the fiscal side, the deficit was contained and the growth of spending tackled. Attention then turned to the framework. Here a long-run focus was provided, so that neither debt nor unfunded liabilities could accumulate unobserved and undiscussed. The 'present and projected budgetary position' has to be published regularly. These changes were contained in the Fiscal Responsiblity Act (of 1994). Dr Brash gives considerable attention to this Act, which is fortunate for it has lessons for elsewhere; not least because while it does not tie government's hands in any way it ensures that there can be no concealment of either deeds or plans. The Act provides 'transparency'.

The monetary policy changes are well known and widely discussed. A response to fairly drastic monetary mismanagement, they commit the government to low inflation (unless it openly backs away from that objective), and let the central bank get on with achieving and maintaining that objective. The New Zealand dollar was floated in 1985, and has remained freely floating.

After describing these numerous changes, Dr Brash concludes by discussing 'Where to From Here?'. In that discussion he makes important points of general interest. Before concluding this Preface by noting these, two other issues are well worth considering briefly.

Lessons for Economic Policy Reform

Although New Zealand's reforms have received much attention, it is not the only country to have started such a programme. From the experience of these countries, two questions are often raised. Why does reform eventually start? And, if reform is painful in the short run, and for some groups, how can these temporary or sectoral problems be stopped from impeding reform? These questions fall in the domain of what is sometimes called the 'political economy of policy reform'.[2]

New Zealand seems to confirm that reform eventually starts when the situation is bad enough – that a crisis is necessary to allow the process to start. The trouble with that popular and persuasive hypothesis is that it is hard to see how it can ever be wrong. After all, if reform has not started, then plainly the crisis is

---

[2] An extensive discussion of those issues is to be found in Dani Rodrik, 'Understanding Economic Policy Reform', *Journal of Economic Literature,* Vol. XXXIV, No. 1, March 1996.

not yet sufficiently severe. Despite the efforts of political scientists as well as economists, we are not yet far advanced in understanding why reform starts.

New Zealand does, however, provide help on the second question. Dr Brash discusses this point (p.22). Briefly, the answer is that rapid reform over a wide area helps to make the sometimes painful process less painful and therefore more acceptable – through the benefits of one reform compensating for the pains of another, through spreading the burden widely rather than letting one sector suffer, and confounding '...the efforts of vested interests to coalesce against further reform' (p.22).

In summary, complicated compensation plans need not be devised; going at the job rapidly and over a wide range produces its own rough-and-ready, but effective, compensation.

Lessons for the UK

To see the full range of lessons for UK policy it is certainly necessary to read Dr Brash's lecture. But there are two points that should be highlighted. These relate to fiscal and to monetary policy. The Fiscal Responsibility Act would be well worth copying. It embodies some basic principles of responsible fiscal policy, which no government should wish to ignore. The Act recognises that the greatest threat to fiscal responsibility is not malevolence or stupidity, but an unthinking and short-sighted desire to do good. Adopting such an Act would make it harder for the pleas of special interests to damage, either immediately or in the longer term, the prosperity of the economy as a whole.

The benefits from changing Britain's present monetary policy framework would also be considerable. The present Government deserves great credit for opening up monetary policy-making and committing itself to low inflation. But the financial markets are still not entirely convinced. A depoliticisation of monetary policy's operations, along with political choice of their objective as is appropriate in a democracy, can be achieved by copying the Reserve Bank Act. It is hard to see why we do not do so.

There is also a general point, concerning the openness of government. Dr Brash touches on that at several points in his lecture, most forcefully and in greatest detail in his conclusion. It is appropriate to move finally to that.

Conclusion

At the end of his lecture, Dr Brash considers where else New Zealand can reform. He discusses not details of individual policies, but rather the approach to reform. He emphasises just how important it is to *explain* – to explain what the benefits of reform are, how they come about, and why the process is desirable. The last may seem obvious – it makes people better off both now and in the future. But there is more to it than that.

> 'The best security against the reversal of recent reforms is to continue with reform in order to encourage growth and employment, and to provide increasing opportunities for the unskilled and those on low incomes to raise both their skills and their incomes...it is actual growth and prosperity, not ideas about the market, that maintain popular support for a free society' (p.47).

Individual liberty is a goal of great importance. Economic growth and prosperity remove a threat to individual freedom; so long as economies are healthy, 'emergency measures' to put things right cannot be imposed. Economic liberalism, as well as bringing prosperity, helps protect freedom. In this lucid, thorough and forceful lecture, Donald Brash demonstrates that point with great clarity. It is a lesson from New Zealand not just for the UK, but for the whole world. This lecture and the reforms it describes demand the attention of electorates and policy-makers worldwide.

November 1996
GEOFFREY E. WOOD
Professor of Economics,
City University Business School, London

The Author

DR. DONALD T. BRASH was born in New Zealand in 1940. He attended Christchurch Boys' High School and Canterbury University, completing a Bachelor of Arts Degree with a double major in economics and history.

In 1962 he obtained his Master of Arts degree with first class honours, majoring in economics. In 1966, Dr. Brash obtained a PhD in economics from the Australian National University, with a thesis on American investment in Australian industry (subsequently published by Harvard University Press).

He served with the World Bank in Washington (1966-71) before becoming Chief Executive of a New Zealand merchant bank (1971-1981), the New Zealand Kiwifruit Authority (1982-86), and the Trust Bank Group (1986-88). He was appointed Governor of the Reserve Bank of New Zealand in September 1988.

Dr. Brash was a member of the New Zealand Monetary and Economic Council from 1974 to 1978; a member of the Committee of Inquiry into Inflation Accounting in 1975; Chairman of the Economic Monitoring Group, 1978-80; a Foundation member of the New Zealand Planning Council; Chairman of the advisory panel on the Goods and Services Tax, 1985; and Chairman of four subsequent consultative committees on taxation reform, on behalf of the New Zealand Government.

New Zealand's Remarkable Reforms

Donald T. Brash*

Governor, Reserve Bank of New Zealand

1. The Recovery of New Zealand

THE REVIVAL OF NEW ZEALAND'S ECONOMY in the last few years follows one of the most remarkable economic liberalisations of modern times, which is often dated from 1984. That is not entirely fair. There were significant steps towards liberalisation in the early 1980s, with the signing of the Closer Economic Relations treaty with Australia and moves towards deregulation of the road transport industry.

But it is certainly true that the process accelerated sharply following the election of a new Labour Government in 1984. Since 15 July 1984, when, just one day after the election of that government, a foreign exchange crisis forced the Reserve Bank to suspend trading in foreign exchange, New Zealand has been transformed from one of the most regulated economies in the OECD to arguably the least regulated. A poll of 10 leading economists in *The Economist* a few months ago ranked New Zealand as the 'freest' of the 20 countries surveyed,[1] while the Fraser Institute's *Economic Freedom of the World: 1975-1995* ranked it third out of 103, with a score of 8 out of 10 (behind Hong Kong with 9·2 and Singapore with 8·2).[2] The *1996 World Competitiveness Report* also ranked New Zealand as the third most competitive economy of the 48 surveyed.[3]

---

* I acknowledge the assistance of Dr Michael James in the preparation of this lecture.

[1] *The Economist*, 13 January 1996, p. 21.

[2] James Gwartney, Robert Lawson and Walter Block, *Economic Freedom of the World: 1975-1995*, Vancouver BC: Fraser Institute, 1996 (available from the IEA).

[3] World Economic Forum, *1996 World Competitiveness Report*, Geneva, 1996.

It was not always certain that the reforms would succeed. After growing at half the average OECD rate between 1950 and 1984, New Zealand's economy went into virtual hibernation during the reform years of 1985 to 1992. But in 1993, the growth rate rose swiftly to 5·6 per cent, and in 1994 it was 6·2 per cent: the fastest growth rates in the OECD during this two-year period.

The most impressive indicator of recovery, however, has been unemployment. After reaching a peak of nearly 11 per cent in 1991, it has fallen rapidly over the last few years and is now down to 6·2 per cent overall, and only 4·6 per cent for New Zealanders of European origin. (Unfortunately, unemployment among Maoris and Pacific Islanders remains much higher, at more than 15 per cent.) Meanwhile inflation, which a decade ago was over 15 per cent, has been between 0 and 2 per cent for almost all of the last five years. Private sector investment has risen very strongly and, while growth in investment has slowed down over the last year, remains at historically high levels. Central government spending has fallen from over 41 per cent of GDP in the early 1990s to around 35 per cent today, while net government debt has fallen from a peak of 52 per cent of GDP in 1992 to around 33 per cent today.

Economic Growth Now Sustainable

Although economic growth has slowed over the last year, and inflation has risen marginally above 2 per cent, New Zealand's recovery seems sustainable. The Reserve Bank estimates that sustainable real GDP growth of between 3 and 3·5 per cent is now possible in New Zealand and, while this is clearly much slower than our growth in the very recent past (and lower than the sustainable growth estimates of some other commentators), it is markedly better than the growth of which we were capable prior to the reforms, and better also than the sustainable growth of which other mature OECD economies now seem capable. In 1996 and 1997, New Zealanders are due to receive tax cuts that increase disposable incomes by between 6 and 8 per cent over that period. Since these cuts will be financed from substantial and structural budget surpluses, they represent true dividends of growth, not borrowings from future generations.

This apparent success story has generated renewed interest in the reforms that have radically reshaped New Zealand's economy.

The New Zealand case provides impressive *prima facie* evidence that micro-economic reform and macro-economic stability are keys to higher growth rates and rising living standards. It also contains some lessons about how economic reform should be conducted and about the political conditions that make for its successful implementation.

2. Hayek and New Zealand

FRIEDRICH VON HAYEK, the man in whose memory this lecture is given, appears to have visited New Zealand only once, briefly, and never referred to it in his writings. I have not attempted to determine how many of those who were crucial in designing and implementing the reforms had read Hayek prior to the mid-1980s, but I rather suspect that not many had. In a recent speech, Lindsay Perigo, a New Zealand journalist, referred to New Zealand as 'a country reformed by Hayekians, run by pragmatists, and populated by socialists'.[4] But while, as I will explain in a moment, the New Zealand reforms have a distinctly Hayekian flavour, I am not at all sure how conscious of Hayek most of the architects actually were.

I myself was not involved in the earliest stages of the reform process, but became heavily involved in the taxation and monetary policy aspects of it at a fairly early stage. And like many of my peers, I had been brought up on an undiluted diet of Keynesian economics and an almost undiluted diet of Fabian socialist politics. Although doing undergraduate study at the University of Canterbury in Christchurch in the late 1950s, I was almost totally unaware that Karl Popper had written one of the most important books in the evolution of economic liberalism (*The Open Society and its Enemies*) at the same university not 15 years earlier. I well recall the dismay, indeed incredulity, I felt when I first visited the United States in 1959 and met some people who were opposed to Keynesian deficit financing. I admit with acute embarrassment that, until invited to give this lecture, I had not read any of Hayek's writings. My own abandonment of Keynesian economics and Fabian socialism was not, therefore, the result of reading Hayek, Popper or even Friedman but of the gradual recognition

---

[4] 'The Antipodean Tea-Party', reprinted in *The Free Radical*, April/May 1996, p. 16.

that neither Keynesian economics nor Fabian socialism actually worked in the way their originators intended. I suspect that the same is true of many of those who were the real architects of the New Zealand reform process.[5] Yet much about the story of New Zealand's decline and recovery has a Hayekian flavour. I want to comment on four aspects in particular.

New Zealand's Economic Decline – Hayek's 'Baleful Logic'

First of all, the decline of New Zealand after the Second World War displayed the baleful logic of Hayek's road to serfdom. In the late 1930s, New Zealand was, as now, an object of international interest; but then it was as a pioneer of 'cradle-to-grave' welfare. In addition, New Zealand erected protective trade barriers and price, wage and capital controls in an attempt to insulate itself from changes in the world economy and to suppress inflation. But each intervention created distortions that spawned new interventions. By the early 1980s, almost all prices, interest rates, rents, wages, and dividends were controlled by government – to say nothing of import controls and foreign exchange controls. The result was a sort of serfdom, not the police-state and concentration-camp variety that dominated Europe as Hayek was composing *The Road to Serfdom*, but the bureaucratic kind that was described with startling foresight by Alexis de Tocqueville in *Democracy in America* (published in 1835), whose vision of democratic totalitarianism so impressed Hayek.

Tocqueville said that

'the supreme power ... covers the surface of society with a network of small complicated rules, minute and uniform, through which the most

---

5   I suspect this is also true of the direct influence of the Chicago School. There is a view in New Zealand that the reforms were driven by 'Chicago'. It is certainly true that Friedman's *Free to Choose* was read widely in New Zealand when it first came out, and was screened on television. I myself was involved in inviting Friedman to make his first visit to New Zealand in 1981. But to the best of my knowledge none of those most closely involved in the reform process ever studied at Chicago. In fact, the most common academic background of those involved in the reform process was probably the University of Canterbury – in the late 1980s, the Secretary of the Treasury, one of the Deputy Secretaries of the Treasury, the Governor of the Reserve Bank, the Minister of Finance, and the Opposition Shadow Finance Minister were all graduates of Canterbury, and three of the five had been to the same state-funded secondary school! None of the five had studied at Chicago, and only one had studied in the US.

original minds and most energetic characters cannot penetrate, to rise above the crowd. The will of man is not shattered but softened, bent, and guided; men are seldom forced by it to act, but they are constantly restrained from acting: such a power does not destroy, but it prevents existence; it does not tyrannise, but it compresses, enervates, extinguishes, and stupefies a people, till each nation is reduced to be nothing better than a flock of timid and industrious animals, of which the government is the shepherd. ...I have always thought that servitude of the regular, quiet and gentle kind which I have just described might be combined more easily than is commonly believed with some of the outward forms of freedom, and that it might even establish itself under the wing of the sovereignty of the people.'[6]

This description could have applied with not much qualification to New Zealand in the 1970s and, even more clearly, in the early 1980s. Roger (now Sir Roger) Douglas, Minister of Finance in the Labour Government between 1984 and late 1988 and architect of the first wave of reform, recalls the description given by a businessman, Bob Matthew. Among many other things, you needed exchange control approval to subscribe to a foreign journal, you needed a doctor's prescription to buy margarine, and only two sorts of refrigerator were available – both made by the same manufacturer and to the same specifications.[7] Richard Prebble, Minister for State-Owned Enterprises in the same government, tells an anecdote that encapsulates the effects of such regulation on a society. New Zealand Rail lost a tractor as it was being transported from one town to another. The owner, despairing of getting any satisfaction from the railways, went looking for it himself. A week later, he found it in a siding along with six wagons the railways had also lost.[8]

The Crisis of 1984

The response to the crisis of 1984 also has a Hayekian ring. It involved a spectacular collapse of the mental defences against the intellectual counter-revolution which Hayek had begun in the 1940s and which since the mid-1970s had been rapidly gaining

---

6   A. De Tocqueville, *Democracy in America*, Vol. 1 1835, Vol. 2 1840, ed. J.P. Mayer, trans. G. Lawrence, New York: Doubleday, 1969.

7   Roger Douglas, *Unfinished Business*, Auckland: Random House, 1993, p.257.

8   Richard Prebble, *I've Been Thinking*, Auckland: Seaview Publishing, 1996, p.7.

ground against the collectivist orthodoxy. This was an unusually exciting time, intellectually speaking, in New Zealand. The economic debate brought together a small but strategically influential team of civil servants, think-tankers, policy-makers and politicians around Roger Douglas. This group of quite remarkable people understood clearly what needed to be done and was committed to seeing it through.

As should become clear in more detail below, the reforms reflected Hayek's view of the market-place as a 'discovery procedure'. This is the second Hayekian aspect of the reforms I want to stress. The market reforms that have swept the world over the last two decades largely reflect the intellectual influence of neo-classical economics, in particular the Chicago School variety, which emphasises the superiority of the market over central planning as an allocator of resources. New Zealand was influenced by this too (though in the indirect way I have described above). But the rather different view of Hayek, and the Austrian School generally, of the market as a discovery procedure, which stresses the importance of information flows, is manifest in particular in the reforms of New Zealand's public sector. We have sought to make the operations of the public sector as transparent as possible, so that information about it can be acquired at low cost, and economic decisions thereby rendered more rational and efficient. The most innovative of New Zealand's reforms – the ones that arguably make the country a world leader in reform – are the Public Finance Act, the Reserve Bank Act, and the Fiscal Responsibility Act. These reforms impart to the market a steady flow of information about the assets and liabilities of the state and about the conduct of both monetary policy and fiscal policy.

The Rule of Law

The third and fourth Hayekian themes in the New Zealand story reflect the shift of emphasis in Hayek's later work away from pure economics and towards jurisprudential and constitutional issues, as Hayek became increasingly concerned about the institutional underpinnings of a free society. In *The Constitution of Liberty* (1960), he promoted a conception of the rule of law as the enforcement of a uniform set of rules of conduct across society as a whole, without favouring or discriminating against any special interests. The implication for economic policy was that no sectors of the economy should be singled out for special treatment, whether in the form of favours like tariff protection or subsidies, or in the form of burdens like industry-specific levies and controls.

The rule of law is reflected in many New Zealand reforms, but particularly in three areas: industry policy, taxation, and industrial relations. Industry policy comes under the Commerce Act of 1986, which is informed by a notion of contestability that recognises the efficacy of *potential* competition rather than imposing *actual* competition. It provides for a system of general and 'light-handed' industry regulation that to a very great extent places the public and private sectors on the same footing and minimises (without completely excluding) the rôle of 'market dominance' considerations in competition policy. Similarly, international investors have virtually the same degree of access to the New Zealand economy as domestic investors. As for the tax reforms, the flattening and lowering of income-tax rates approaches, though it does not fully realise, the flat (or 'proportional') tax that Hayek advocated as the requirement of the rule of law in this area. The industrial relations reform, meanwhile, brings the labour market under the rule of law by largely (though not completely) subjecting it to the law of contract and by removing the monopoly right of trade unions to workforce representation.

The final Hayekian theme I want to highlight is articulated in *Law, Legislation and Liberty* (1974-79), where Hayek grounded his theory of the rule of law in an ancient conception of justice that reflected principles of higher law and was contradicted by modern notions of 'social' or 'distributive' justice. He also advanced a constitutional scheme, involving an upper house of Parliament, that he hoped would ensure that legislation routinely observed the principles of the rule of law. It has to be said that New Zealand has made little progress in these respects. The welfare state remains little changed, reflecting the continuing currency in New Zealand of modern, collectivist notions of social justice. Some constitutional change has been effected, but it is far from clear that it brings New Zealand much closer to a genuine 'constitution of liberty' in Hayek's terms. I shall return to these themes later.

3. The Reform Process

THE COMPREHENSIVE NATURE OF THE ECONOMIC POLICY FAILURE in New Zealand demanded a correspondingly comprehensive reform programme. As well, the first stage of the reform was carried out at high speed. It was probably the world's first example of a 'big bang' approach to reform. The case for fast and comprehensive, as opposed to gradual and piecemeal, action was cogently argued by Roger Douglas in a remarkable speech to a meeting of the Mont Pelèrin Society in Christchurch in 1989.[9] Douglas rejected the conventional view that reform can succeed only if political support for it has been established beforehand; this, he said, merely compromised the quality of the reforms, thus adding to their eventual cost and sowing the seeds of opposition. Instead, he said, consensus 'develops progressively after the decisions are implemented, as they deliver satisfactory outcomes to the public'.

Douglas went on to spell out a number of guidelines for successful reform. One important guideline was the need to implement reforms in quantum leaps and to continue doing so until the reform programme was completed. He argued that this approach had three advantages.

- *First*, the cost of reforming each sector of the economy was quickly compensated by the benefits flowing from the reform of the other sectors, thus generating support for the completion of the programme.

- *Second*, rapid reform retained the initiative in the hands of government and confounded the efforts of vested interests to coalesce against further reform: 'Opponents' fire is much less accurate if they have to shoot at a rapidly moving target.'

- *Third*, rapid reform on a broad front spread the burden of reform equitably, thus enhancing the legitimacy and the acceptability of the programme.

---

9   Reproduced as 'The Politics of Reform: The Art of the Possible', Ch.10 in Roger Douglas, *op. cit.*

It is fair to say that Roger Douglas did not have the opportunity fully to apply and test this strategy. True, his reforms were well received at the time. The 1984 financial crisis gave him the opportunity to take radical action. The deregulation of the financial system was welcomed by the finance industry itself. As well, some of the groups disadvantaged by the early reforms responded by urging further reforms. The farming sector in particular, deprived of its subsidies at a stroke at the very beginning of the reform process, strongly supported faster tariff cuts; and both farmers and manufacturers called for public spending reductions in order to reduce pressure on real interest rates and the exchange rate.

The Labour Government was re-elected in 1987 with an increased majority. Yet it felt unable to tackle the deregulation of the labour market and the continuing rapid growth of government services. Indeed, this constraint probably helped maintain popular support for the early liberalisations, even though Labour Party resistance to further reform forced Roger Douglas to resign in late 1988, about a year after he proposed a flat-rate income tax. But the result was that both wages and public spending continued to rise rapidly in the late 1980s; there can be little doubt this aggravated the effects of the recession of the early 1990s, so weakening public support for further reform. Nevertheless, the National Government elected in 1990 pressed on with the programme that Labour had left incomplete: unburdened by any institutional links with the trade union movement, it deregulated the labour market, made some reductions in welfare benefits, and generally brought public spending under control. The Bolger Government was re-elected in 1993, but with a majority of only one.

Although New Zealanders remain ambivalent about, and even in some respects hostile to, the upheaval of the last 12 years, opinion polls suggest that they agree in increasing numbers, now a majority, that the country is 'on the right track'. Encouragingly, most of them now support the labour market reforms. An interesting contrast can be drawn with the United States, where, although the Congress reliably delivers benefits to the special interests it represents, the population increasingly feels their country is 'on the wrong track'. If people can distinguish between their particular interests and the general interest, there is scope for political leadership to win support for further reform.

4. The Reforms

THE EXTENT OF THE REFORMS IN NEW ZEALAND was so great that it is difficult to describe them in short compass. They were both micro-economic (concerned with the efficient allocation of resources through improvements in the way the price and incentive system operates in individual markets) and macro-economic (concerned with the whole environment within which producers and consumers make their choices). Among the micro-economic changes were sweeping moves to liberalise international trade and deregulate markets; fundamental reform of the taxation system; some measures to reform the delivery of income support, health and education; extensive moves to improve the efficiency of core government departments; and the corporatisation and privatisation of many government trading activities. In the macro-economic arena, changes in the approach to both fiscal and monetary policy were far-reaching.

Micro-Reforms

(i) Market Liberalisation

Finance: Some of the earliest reforms were in the financial sector. All controls on prices, wages, credit, dividends, foreign exchange and out-bound overseas investment were lifted in 1984, and the New Zealand dollar was floated early in 1985. Banks were freed from any quantitative limits on their lending growth. The requirement for banks to hold deposits with the central bank, or to hold specified investments in government securities, was abolished. Banking, previously the exclusive preserve of one government-owned institution and three foreign-owned banks, was opened up to full competition. The licensing of those authorised to deal in foreign exchange was discontinued. Competition between currencies, which Hayek recommended in the 1970s,[10] was given some scope in that contracts could be denominated in any cur-

---

[10] F.A. Hayek, *Denationalisation of Money – The Argument Refined*, Hobart Paper ('Special') No.70, London: Institute of Economic Affairs, 1976, 3rd Edn., 1990.

rency (though taxes must still be paid in New Zealand dollars, and the Customs Act prohibits the importation of other currencies intended for circulation).

In January 1996, the banking system was further liberalised when the Reserve Bank commenced a rather different way of conducting prudential supervision. Instead of reporting on a confidential basis to the central bank, banks are now required to issue detailed quarterly public disclosure statements, which must be audited twice-yearly by external auditors. Instead of limiting their exposure to individual counter-parties to some central-bank-specified percentage of capital, banks must simply disclose how much risk concentration they have in their portfolio at end of quarter, and at peak intra-quarter. Instead of complying with detailed guidelines on internal controls, directors must simply attest, in the quarterly disclosure statements, that the internal controls are appropriate to the nature of the banking business being undertaken.

Trade: Quantitative import licensing was completely phased out by the early 1990s. Tariffs have been progressively reduced since 1984; the present phase aims to cut tariffs on almost all products to 5 percent by 2000, with a further major review of tariffs scheduled for 1998 to determine when to move to free trade. The Closer Economic Relations agreement with Australia, inaugurated in 1983 before the major parts of the reform programme began, as mentioned above, aims to establish complete freedom of trans-Tasman trade and investment and has substantially accomplished that already. As a member of the Asia-Pacific Economic Community (APEC), New Zealand is committed to free trade and investment in the Asia-Pacific region by 2020. One of the advantages of being small on the international stage is that one is not tempted to delay liberalisation in the hope of extracting some 'reciprocal' liberalisation from others. We have far too little bargaining power to make that game sensible (if indeed it ever is), so that most of our trade liberalisation has been unilateral. In other words, we have liberalised our importing not because we have been forced to do so by others, but because successive governments have recognised that it is in New Zealand's own interests to do so.

Agriculture and Industry: Agricultural and industrial subsidies, whether for export or for other activities, were virtually abolished at a very early stage. Monopolies in domestic air services, tight restrictions on long-distance road transport (designed to protect the government-owned railway monopoly), quantitative licensing of the taxi industry, the reservation to domestic shipping of the coastal trade, the prohibition on private sector electricity generation, the restriction on courier services (designed to protect the Post Office), and the tight constraint on telecommunications – all have been abolished, as have previously tight restrictions on shop-trading hours. Occupational licensing has been ended in a number of professions and trades. Domestic investors enjoy no regulatory advantage over foreign investors.

A conspicuous exception to this deregulatory pattern is the marketing of some agricultural exports – exports of dairy products, apples, pears and kiwifruit, making up some 17 per cent of total merchandise exports in 1995, are still under the control of statutory marketing boards.

Research and Development: Early on in the reform programme, research and development was placed on an equal footing with other forms of investment by the abolition of R&D concessions, and public R&D work was subjected to cost-recovery arrangements. In 1990, a pool of contestable funds for R&D was set up, and government research bodies (Crown Research Institutes) corporatised two years later.

The Labour Market: Perhaps the most remarkable liberalisation was that of the labour market. The Labour Governments of 1984-90 upheld compulsory unionism[11] and did little to change the centralised nature of wage-fixing in New Zealand, although the nature of wage-bargaining was certainly changed both by the phasing down of border protection and by the Government's refusal to continue a long-established tradition of getting directly involved in major industrial disputes. The National Government's Employment Contracts Act 1991, however, placed labour contracts on almost the same basis as other commercial contracts. Each employer has a written employment contract with every employee; the contract may be a set of individual contracts or a collective contract (or a combination of both). Employees may

---

11 Indeed, the Labour Government reinstated compulsory unionism – it had been abolished shortly before the National Government was defeated in 1984.

choose their own bargaining agents; trade unions may act as bargaining agents, but have no special legal standing (other than being exempt from competition law). The Act lays down procedures for settling disputes, although the parties to a contract may use different procedures if they all agree.

The deregulation is not complete. The Act provides for certain minimum entitlements that must be observed in employment contracts, including a minimum wage, minimum holiday entitlements, parental leave and equal pay for men and women. In addition, the Act provides for an Employment Court to settle labour disputes, which may, however, like other disputes, be appealed to the Appeal Court.

But the Employment Contracts Act has rapidly promoted the use of enterprise bargaining and individual contracts. The proportion of the workforce on individual or collective enterprise-specific contracts has increased dramatically, while by December 1995 only 17 per cent of the workforce was covered by union-negotiated collective contracts.

Working days lost through strikes have also declined sharply. In 1990, the last full year prior to the enactment of the Employment Contracts Act, working days lost through work stoppages amounted to 331,000. In 1994, the last full year for which data is available and a year in which the economy was growing strongly, the loss was only 38,000 days. Does that perhaps overstate the change? On average, over the eight calendar years prior to the enactment of the new law (1983 to 1990), days lost to work stoppages were 519,000 per annum. Over the next four years (1991 to 1994), the annual average was 69,000 – a dramatic change in any language.

But the most encouraging evidence of the success of the Employment Contracts Act is that the subsequent rise in the rate of productivity growth has not been achieved at the expense of employment: on the contrary, as already noted, unemployment has fallen rapidly over the last few years, while numbers employed have increased at an average of some 3·3 per cent per annum since 1991.

(ii) Taxation

Prior to its reform, the New Zealand tax system was an awful mess judged by almost any standard. Personal income taxes were ostensibly steeply progressive, reaching a top marginal rate of 66 per cent, but that rate was reached at such a relatively low level of income (NZ$38,000 per annum) that avoidance and evasion were widespread with resultant loss of revenue and considerable misallocation of investment (to take advantage of tax shelters). Wholesale sales taxes were widely used, but varied from very low rates to 50 per cent, with the higher tax rates sometimes applying to items for no better reason than that they did not form part of the CPI regimen, and so would not adversely affect the measured inflation rate. Over the last decade, New Zealand's tax system has been fundamentally simplified and reformed, with a view to broadening the tax base and flattening the tax scale.

In 1986 all wholesale sales taxes were abolished, and replaced with a broad-based value-added tax (the Goods and Services Tax) with a single rate of 10 per cent (raised in 1989 to 12·5 per cent). The unusual thing about that tax is that the Government was willing to include everything except financial services in the tax net – food, medical services, books, children's clothing, the lot – all at the same rate, recognising that only by so doing would economic distortions be avoided and the compliance costs entailed in collecting the tax be minimised. At the same time, cuts were made in the rate of income tax: the five-rate scale was cut to three rates of 15, 30 and 48 per cent, and replaced in 1988 with a two-rate scale of 24 and 33 per cent (though the effect of a low-earner rebate is to convert this scale effectively into a three-step scale of 15, 28, and 33 per cent). The company tax rate was reduced from 48 to 33 per cent, in recognition of the desirability of having the company tax rate equal to the top personal rate, and an imputation credit system was introduced for dividends to do away with the previous double taxation of distributed company income. Estate taxes were abolished in 1992.

To broaden the income-tax base, some new taxes were introduced: a Fringe Benefits Tax in 1985 to put all forms of remuneration, both in cash and in kind, on the same tax basis, and a resident withholding tax on interest and dividend income in 1989. In addition, many income tax concessions, including those on life insurance and superannuation, were abolished. (New Zealand has never had a deduction for mortgage interest payments, so common in many other countries, so that was not

[28]

available to be abolished.) Scope for tax avoidance by companies was also substantially reduced.

The overall effect of these measures has been to reduce the proportion of tax revenues derived from income taxes, though this remains more than half. In addition, the share of total tax revenue paid by wage and salary earners fell from 64 to 40 per cent between 1983/84 and 1994/95, while that for companies and the self-employed rose. Perhaps most important for our present purposes, the OECD has described New Zealand's present tax structure as probably the least distorting of any in an OECD country.

Earlier this year, income tax cuts were announced. The 24 per cent tax rate was reduced to 21·5 per cent as from 1 July 1996 and to 19·5 per cent a year later. The 33 per cent rate remains, but the threshold will be substantially raised in two stages in 1996 and 1997. Interestingly, the Government deliberately sought to reduce the tax on those with relatively low levels of earned income, partly no doubt to reflect the fact that this group has been relatively slow to share in the benefits of the growing economy in recent years but partly also in an attempt to widen the gap between those in low-wage employment and those on benefits. Those primarily dependent on benefits will in fact receive relatively little from the planned tax cuts.

(iii) Income Support, Education and Health

Although New Zealand's welfare state has undergone some reform – and given the almost total absence of significant reform of welfare states elsewhere that is itself a considerable accomplishment – it has not been subjected to the kind of radical restructuring which the rest of the economy has experienced. The changes have been designed mainly to contain the growth in spending on government services and benefits by targeting them more directly at areas of greatest need, and to improve the per-formance of government agencies, rather than to place them on a market or quasi-market footing.

Income Support: Nearly a quarter of New Zealanders receive a state-funded pension or a benefit. The main cause of the increase in spending on income support over the last two decades has been the National Superannuation scheme, which accounts for over half the cost of all income support programmes. When introduced in 1977, the scheme provided state-funded superannuation to everyone of at least 60 years of age, to a value of 80 per cent of average weekly earnings for married couples. In 1979 the benefit was indexed to net rather than gross wages, and in 1985 a 20 per cent surcharge was imposed on recipients' other income. In 1991, the Government announced that the age of eligibility would be progressively increased to 65 by 2002, that the value of the pension for married couples would be adjusted by the CPI until it declined to 65 per cent of the average after-tax wage, and that the surcharge would be increased to 25 per cent.

Also in 1991, most benefits other than National Superannuation were cut by between 5 and 27 per cent, and automatic indexation to the CPI abolished. Unemployment benefit was denied to 16 and 17-year-olds, youth rates extended to age 24, and the stand-down period extended, up to a maximum of 26 weeks in cases of voluntary resignation. The universal family benefit was abolished and replaced by a selective scheme paid to families with dependent children, means-tested according to parental income. Child support legislation rendered non-custodial parents of children up to age 19 liable for a maintenance payment based on numbers of children and the non-custodial parent's gross income. The payment is used to help fund the Domestic Purposes Benefit if the custodial parent is receiving it; otherwise it is paid directly to the custodial parent.

But, despite the reforms, and despite a surprisingly widespread perception that the 1991 changes 'abolished the welfare state in New Zealand', spending on income support remains very substantial. In the year to March 1990, the net fiscal impact of social welfare expenditure amounted to $9,510 million, or 13·6 per cent of GDP. In the year to June 1995, the net fiscal impact was still $10,101 million, or 11·5 per cent of GDP, virtually unchanged from the percentage of GDP spent on income support in the year to March 1985 (11·3 per cent). The number of people receiving the Domestic Purposes Benefit, which is payable to single parents, to women without dependent children and no other means of support, and to full-time carers of disabled persons, stood at 17,231 in 1975; by June 1990, this figure had increased to 94,823 and by June 1995 to 104,027. About a quarter of all families with children are headed by a sole parent; two out of every five births today are ex-nuptial. Whereas in 1975, 9,414 people were in receipt of the Invalids Benefit, in 1990 the figure was 27,824 and in 1995 39,686. One could be excused for assuming that New Zealand has recently been involved in some major war!

Housing: For many years, successive governments provided subsidised housing and mortgages as a way of assisting low-income people into housing. These subsidies have now been replaced by an accommodation supplement in the form of a cash grant or housing voucher. It is available to all low-income house-holds, whether they live in state-owned houses or are renting or buying private houses. Although a relatively controversial measure, it appears to have provided significantly greater housing choice for many low-income families, and to have compelled the government as landlord for some low-income people to improve the quality of its housing.

Education: School management (with the exception of control of salary budgets) was devolved to school boards of trustees in the late 1980s. Over the last few years, there has been an attempt to devolve control of salary budgets also but this has met determined resistance from the union representing secondary school teachers and to date less than 10 per cent of state-funded secondary schools control their own salary budgets (tertiary institutions, however, have a much higher degree of financial autonomy now than a decade ago). Centrally determined zoning was abolished in 1991.

In tertiary education, tuition fees were introduced in 1990 and will rise to an average of 25 per cent of course costs. Government-guaranteed loans are available to help cover tuition, course and living costs. Repayment is made through the tax system. Selective maintenance and accommodation allowances are available, means-tested against parental income.

Health Care: The most radical welfare reforms have occurred in health care. Their guiding principle has been the separation of the purchasing from the provision of health services. Four regional health authorities have been set up, which use state funds to buy health services for their regions; any provider, including the 23 Crown Health Enterprises (government-owned hospitals), may tender for contracts to supply services. In addition, some user charges have been imposed. Hospital outpatients pay charges at a similar rate to patients of private GPs; part-charges are payable on prescription pharmaceuticals (though these are limited to $3 per prescription for those holding a Community Services Card or a High Use Card – in total about half the population – and are waived entirely for this group after 20 prescriptions per annum).

Between 1991 and 1995, the share of GDP consumed by state spending on income support, education and health fell from 25·8 to 24·5 per cent. In that sense, the reforms may be regarded as having been successful. But it is worthwhile for both supporters and critics to recall that, at present levels, state spending on those activities remains well above the 21·6 per cent of GDP spent in 1983/84.

(iv) Government Departments

The non-trading elements of New Zealand's public sector were reformed by the State Sector Act 1988 and the Public Finance Act 1989, both of which aim to. discipline the bureaucracy by introducing incentives to eliminate the bias towards waste, including the incentives flowing from transparency.

Under the State Sector Act, all appointees to the top positions in government departments and ministries are on term contracts. Department heads, now known as chief executives (CEs), have greater decision-making autonomy than before. They are now, for example, the employer of all the staff in their departments, and so have the power to hire, pay, promote and fire departmental personnel. The State Services Commission selects departmental CEs, so they are non-political appointments.

The Public Finance Act achieves a number of goals. It transfers responsibility for each department's financial operations from the Treasury to departmental CEs, each of whom maintains a departmental account which handles all receipts and payments. Ministers contract with CEs annually for the provision of 'outputs' (specific and measurable tasks) rather than the 'outcomes' (policy objectives) that the outputs are designed to achieve. The agreements are tabled in Parliament. CEs have wide discretion in fulfilling the terms of their agreements; they may produce goods and services internally or may outsource them, and are not required to buy inputs from other government agencies. To some extent at least, their remuneration depends on the efficiency of their departments.

[32]

Perhaps the most innovative provision of the Public Finance Act is that requiring government to move from cash accounting to accrual accounting, based on Generally Accepted Accounting Practice, for the purpose of budgeting and management. Unlike cash accounting, accrual accounting takes account of the value of receivables (amounts due but unpaid), of payables (amounts owed but unpaid), of government assets, and of non-cash obligations such as unfunded pension liabilities. Accrual accounting thus facilitates a more comprehensive assessment than does cash accounting of the state sector's true financial position. The first state sector financial statement (for fiscal year 1992/93) revealed a negative 'net worth' on the part of the Crown of nearly NZ$8 billion. This was undoubtedly one of the factors prompting the changes in fiscal policy which produced a positive net worth in December 1995.

Finally, the Public Finance Act allowed the development of a capital charge system. Twice a year, each department must pay Treasury a capital levy based on the total value of the government's investment in the department and an appropriate interest rate (essentially the before-tax weighted average cost of capital judged appropriate to the business of the department). This charge is designed to encourage departmental CEs to economise on their use of assets, and anecdotal evidence suggests it has been very successful in doing this.[12]

The Reserve Bank is not itself subject to either the State Sector Act or the Public Finance Act, but operates under some of the same principles of accountability within its own legislation. Thus the Reserve Bank of New Zealand Act 1989 deprived the Bank of the automatic right to the seigniorage on currency issue (the source of a very large amount of central bank inefficiency the world over), and instead required the Governor of the Bank to negotiate five-yearly funding agreements with the Minister of Finance for ratification by Parliament. The first such agreement in 1990 fixed the Bank's operating expenses at the level budgeted for the 1990/91 financial year (NZ$56·7 million) for a full five years.

---

[12] As an illustration, the Ministry of Foreign Affairs and Trade has reviewed its policy of owning all of its overseas posts and has decided to sell some of them, and rent equivalent space.

The Minister took the view that if we were committed to delivering price stability, we should prove it. Such was the power of the incentives created by the very public nature of the agreement, in a climate where improving efficiency and effectiveness were definitely regarded as desirable, that in the fifth year covered by the agreement, 1994/95, operating expenses were only NZ$35·1 million, 38 per cent below the allowed limit. The funding agreement under which the Bank now operates means that, even in 1999/2000, operating expenses should be under NZ$40 million, despite the Bank incurring one or two major new expenditures, such as that entailed in operating a real-time gross settlements system. Bank staff levels, at under 300, are today little more than half those of six years ago.

(v) Corporatisation and Privatisation

When the reform process began in the mid-1980s, the New Zealand government provided a very large range of goods and services which in many other predominantly market economies are supplied by the private sector. Thus, for example, government owned the largest bank, several quasi-banks (Development Finance Corporation, Rural Bank, Post Office Savings Bank),[13] the only domestic airline, an international shipping line, the only railway, all electricity generation and distribution facilities, the dominant producer of coal, the largest forest resource, and the only telecommunications company; to say nothing of the operations which are more generally provided by the public service in other countries, such as the Post Office. Many of these operations were extremely inefficient by international standards, and provided poor levels of service. Despite their monopoly positions, many were a substantial drain on the public purse: the state coal operations, for example, had, by 1986, made a loss in each of the previous 20 years.

Over the course of the late 1980s, these operations were to undergo sweeping change, which would have the effect of hugely improving their performance by any measure.

---

[13] In fact, in the mid-1980s, the government owned or guaranteed financial institutions accounting for more than half the total assets of all M3 institutions.

[34]

The State-Owned Enterprises Act 1986

One of the major pieces of legislation effecting this change was the State-Owned Enterprises Act 1986, which provided the basis for converting state commercial entities into state-owned enterprises (SOEs) operating under the same conditions as private sector enterprises, including the need to raise capital on the open market without government guarantee. (Explicit statements by the Government that state-owned enterprises would be allowed to fail were taken with a grain of salt until late in 1988, when the government-owned Shipping Corporation came close to failing. The Government made it clear that it would not support the Corporation, even if this meant its failure, which prompted its directors to reflag their vessels in Hong Kong and warn New Zealand crew that they had four hours in which to accept an internationally competitive level of manning or be replaced by the Filipinos they could see on the wharf. The resolution of substantial over-manning in this draconian way enabled the Corporation to recover its profitability and, shortly thereafter, it was sold to a British shipping company.)

As noted earlier, the Commerce Act 1986 establishes a common regulatory régime for the trading activities of the public and private sectors by making them both equally open to competition. Its system of 'light-handed' pro-competition regulation eschews industry-specific regulation and allows disputes over the abuse of monopoly power to be referred to the courts. The new competitive régime for SOEs entailed separating their commercial from their non-commercial activities, with the latter being delivered by government departments or purchased directly from the SOEs. Corporatised SOEs have a company form, with the Minister for State-Owned Enterprises as the sole shareholder; their boards of directors are responsible to the Ministers of Finance and of State-Owned Enterprises.

The 14 SOEs corporatised in 1987 achieved some spectacular gains in productivity and profitability. For example, between 1987 and 1990, Telecom reduced staffing levels by 47 per cent, increased productivity by 85 per cent, and increased profits by 300 per cent. Railways cut its freight rates by 50 per cent in real terms between 1983 and 1990, reduced its staff by 60 per cent, and made an operating profit in 1989/90, the first for six years. New Zealand

Post reduced its workforce by 30 per cent, and increased the rate of next-day delivery within the country from 80 to 98 per cent. Coal Corporation increased productivity by 60 per cent and cut its real prices by 20 per cent.

Port Companies Act 1988

New Zealand's ports were also 'corporatised', though since the central government claimed no ownership of these they were not handled through the State-Owned Enterprises Act. Rather, the Government passed the Port Companies Act 1988. This had the effect of creating corporate entities owned by relevant local (municipal) governments, giving them commercially-oriented boards, and encouraging competition between the ports. In addition, the following year the Waterfront Industry Commission was abolished: prior to its abolition, the Commission effectively employed all waterside workers throughout the country. It operated a productivity agreement with employees which effectively rewarded employees according to the increase in tonnage handled. This had the effect of seriously inhibiting investment in new cargo-handling equipment.

The change in culture which followed was little short of extraordinary. The day the Waterfront Industry Commission was abolished, port stevedoring companies offered employment to those people they felt were needed to service the ships, and the balance, roughly 50 per cent of the previous workforce, were paid redundancy. Further staff reductions occurred subsequently, together with major changes in the basis of remuneration, so that today most New Zealand ports pay the same rate of remuneration whether the work is performed in 'normal working hours' or not. The consequence has been that ship turn-around times have fallen dramatically. In Tauranga, for example, it used to take 12 or 13 days, working only 'normal working hours', to load a 27,000 cubic metre cargo of logs onto a vessel, and it took 44 men to do the job. Today, it takes about 30 hours, working around the clock, and takes only four men. Not so long ago, Mr Hugh Fletcher, managing director of one of New Zealand's largest companies, observed that, while it used to cost as much to move a tonne of newsprint across the wharf in Tauranga as it did in Sydney, now it costs only about 25 per cent of the Sydney cost. Not all reductions in cost and manning have been quite so dramatic, but all have been substantial.

Corporatisation to Privatisation

The logic of corporatisation suggested that even better results might be obtained from privatisation, which would remove the residual scope for political interference, expose the SOEs to the disciplines of private-sector monitoring, and make control contestable. Privatisation began in 1987 and by mid-1995 a total of 27 privatisations had raised NZ$13·2 billion in asset sales. About 15 SOEs remain, though one of the largest of these, the Forestry Corporation, has been put up for sale within recent weeks, and another, the Electricity Corporation, has been divided into two units which will start to compete with each other from 1 October 1996.

Two features distinguish the privatisation experience in New Zealand from that in some other countries. *First*, the Government resisted pressure to favour particular bidders or categories of bidders, or to exclude foreign bidders. The policy was that the assets being sold were the property of taxpayers generally, and for this reason it was important to sell them for the best possible price on behalf of taxpayers. No attempt was made therefore to use privatisation to build a political constituency for a 'share-owning democracy', lest the assets had to be sold below their top market price to achieve this result and taxpayers lose out as a consequence.

Second, there was great reluctance to privatise any government-owned corporation which was not already operating in a contestable market at the time of privatisation. This reluctance related, of course, to a recognition that, were a government-owned monopoly to be privatised, a heavy-handed regulatory framework would be necessary to prevent that private monopoly exercising its power to achieve super profits. Thus, Air New Zealand was not privatised until the domestic skies had been deregulated, and Telecom was not privatised until the telecommunications industry had been opened up to competition. With a few minor exceptions, privatisation has, as a consequence of this approach, not been accompanied by regulation over and above that provided under the Commerce Act.

[37]

Privatised corporations have generally performed well, and probably none more 'visibly' than Telecom. Since privatisation in 1990, Telecom has increased after-tax profits from NZ$257 million (in the year to March 1990) to NZ$717 million in the year to March 1996, has reduced the real prices of telephone services to households by an average of more than 21 per cent (and to businesses by 28 per cent), and has hugely improved the range and quality of its service to consumers. It now has a higher proportion of digital-quality lines (98·8 per cent) than in any other telephone system in the world except Hong Kong and, together with its competitors, has created a situation where businesses feel better about the quality of telecommunications in New Zealand than do businesses in any other country.

Macro-Reforms

(vi) Fiscal Policy

In macro-economic policy, many of the changes in micro-policy which have already been described had an important impact – policies of corporatisation and privatisation, for example, helped to reduce fiscal expenditure both directly, through removing the need for regular injections of funding to offset operating losses, and indirectly, through reducing debt service expenditure below the level otherwise required. The abolition of subsidies for agriculture and industry, and the efficiency gains arising from the Public Finance Act, all helped contain the fiscal deficit. Even the tax reforms, widely seen as involving mainly a reduction in income tax rates, assisted because offsetting the reduction in tax rates was a major broadening of the tax base, through the removal of virtually all tax avoidance opportunities. As a consequence, the fiscal deficit, which reached nearly 7 per cent of GDP in 1983/84 as the reform programme began, was gradually reduced so that by 1989/90 it was down to just 1·3 per cent of GDP.

But there was still an incipient fiscal problem. Many types of government expenditure continued to grow so that total government spending was over 41 per cent of GDP at the beginning of this decade, somewhat higher than the ratio in the mid-1980s. The reduction in the deficit in the late 1980s had been accomplished in part by cutting subsidies to agriculture and industry and by efficiency gains in the core public sector, but to a significant extent by increased taxation. With the subsidies gone and the step-adjustment in public sector efficiency already won, the continuing rise in, particularly, government expenditure on transfer payments, health and education was threatening to increase the deficit again or require increased taxation.

The National Government that won office in late 1990 thus inherited increasing levels of state spending, public debt rising towards 52 per cent of GDP (in 1992), and a budget deficit projected to reach 5 per cent of GDP. New Zealand's credit rating, which had already slipped over the 1980s to AA despite all that had been accomplished, and which was downgraded to AA- very early in 1991, would almost certainly have dropped to A+ had action not been taken to contain the growth of spending. This was certainly a major motivation behind the reduction in the rates of some benefits in December 1990. Somewhat later, Ruth Richardson, the Minister of Finance, began work on a legal framework to promote sound fiscal policies, to provide incentives to consider the long-term as well as the short-term consequences of spending decisions, and to remove from future generations the burden of the cost of consumption of the present generation by reducing public sector debt. This legislation was picked up and strengthened by the new Minister, Bill Birch, in late 1993 and he, with Ruth Richardson, by this time Chair of the Parliamentary Finance and Expenditure Committee, guided the Fiscal Responsibility Bill through to enactment in 1994.

Principles of Responsible Fiscal Management

The Act specifies five principles of responsible fiscal management. These are the requirement to:

- achieve a prudent level of public debt;

- once achieved, maintain public debt at a prudent level;

- achieve and maintain levels of Crown net worth that provide a buffer against adverse shocks;

- manage prudently the risks facing the Crown; and

- provide a reasonable degree of stability and predictability on future tax rates.

[39]

As well as prescribing these guidelines, the Act requires governments to publicise regularly the present and projected budgetary position. An annual Budget Policy Statement must be presented to Parliament before 31 March, well before the deadline for the budget. By presenting the Government's intentions for the current budget and for the longer term in the light of the five principles of prudent fiscal management, the Statement helps direct attention away from immediate budgetary pressures and towards the long-term consequences of current policy. A Fiscal Strategy Report at budget time compares actual economic and fiscal information with the intentions set out in the Budget Policy Statement and also with projections based on current policies up to 10 years ahead. Finally, Parliament receives regular economic and fiscal updates. The Policy Statement, Strategy Report and the update tabled at budget time are scrutinised by Parliament's Finance and Expenditure Committee.

The Fiscal Responsibility Act does not define 'a prudent level of debt'. Indeed, it does not tie the hands of government at all. Governments can depart temporarily from the five principles of responsible fiscal management, but the Act requires that the reasons for such departure must be clearly stated, together with an explanation of how and when a return to compliance is expected to be accomplished. Essentially, the Act requires 'transparency'. In other words, it requires government to be honest with the public about the longer-term implications of current budget decisions. In this way, it is a powerful influence favouring fiscally responsible behaviour. It is not coincidental that, less than two years after enactment, the Government has been able to announce the tax cuts of 1996 and 1997 and to confirm that these cuts appear consistent with on-going fiscal surpluses and the ratio of government debt to GDP falling below 30 per cent over the next year. The principles of the Act are to be applied to local government.

(vii) Monetary Policy

Prior to 1984, New Zealand's inflation record had been amongst the poorest in the OECD – not bad by Latin American or East European standards, but poor nonetheless, with inflation above 10 per cent per annum every year through most of the 1970s and early 1980s. The Reserve Bank operated under legislation which required it to consider all manner of real economy objectives and to implement the day-to-day monetary decisions of government. Over the three decades to the mid-1980s, the Bank was clearly among the 'least independent' of central banks, and had an inflation performance to match.

The new Government which came to power in 1984 was determined to eliminate inflation and directed the Bank to achieve that end. It was also keen to put an end to the cynical manipulation of monetary policy for political purposes – manipulation which often succeeded in getting the Government re-elected, but only at the cost of serious damage to the economy. In Roger Douglas's terms, he was keen to 'Muldoon-proof' monetary policy. Accordingly, he asked the Bank and the Treasury to prepare new legislation appropriate to a modern understanding of what monetary policy can actually deliver. The Reserve Bank of New Zealand Act 1989 was the result.

The Reserve Bank of New Zealand Act 1989

This remarkable piece of legislation has no exact parallels anywhere else in the world. Its key principles are:

- While monetary policy does affect the rate of inflation, it cannot be used to engineer a *sustainably* faster rate of economic growth or a *sustainably* higher level of employment.

- In these circumstances, the most sensible rate of inflation for monetary policy to target is price stability, since any other rate of inflation involves both social and economic cost. Hence, Section 8 of the Act gives monetary policy the sole task of 'achieving and maintaining stability in the general level of prices'.

- In a democracy, it is appropriate for the elected government, not bureaucrats, to define 'stability in the general level of prices', and indeed to override that objective if it so chooses. Hence, Section 9 requires a written Policy Targets Agreement to be signed between Minister of Finance and Governor (the well-known 0 to 2 per cent inflation target), which Section 12 allows the Government to override by Order in Council if desired.

- But having specified the objectives, the Government should leave the Bank to *implement* policy without interference from Government, Treasury, or anybody else.

[41]

- With operating independence should go accountability, in the form of a statutory obligation to report to Parliament at least six-monthly, and an ability for the Governor to be dismissed for 'inadequate performance' under the Policy Targets Agreement. (In the New Zealand model, the Policy Targets Agreement is signed by the Governor personally, and it is the Governor who ultimately carries full responsibility for monetary policy – because, as I was told by the Minister when the legislation was being drafted in 1989, the Government did not feel it would be feasible to fire the whole Bank!)

- Since uncertainty entails costs, the objective of monetary policy, and the *modus operandi* of policy implementation, should be as open and transparent as possible.

Once again, the key is transparency. Indeed, chronologically it was the transparency in the Reserve Bank Act which inspired the idea of attempting something similar for fiscal policy. The Government's hands are tied only by the need to make policy intentions absolutely unambiguous to the public – surely a fundamentally sound principle.

Success of the Monetary Framework

The framework has proved very successful. Inflation has been steadily reduced and, as already mentioned, price stability as defined in the current Policy Targets Agreement has been maintained with scarcely a break for almost five years. Inflationary expectations have also been sharply reduced – as most vividly seen in long-term bond yields which have been consistently lower than those in, for example, Australia for some years, and lower than those in the United Kingdom also for most of the last four or five years.

The framework has also been one factor in the trend to much improved fiscal performance – the Government has understood that, for any given inflation target, an easing of fiscal policy involves some tightening of monetary policy. In the 1990 election campaign, the National Opposition promised the public lower interest rates if elected – not by interfering with the implementation of monetary policy but by 'giving monetary policy some mates', in the form of tighter fiscal policy and labour market deregulation. The desire to see an easing in monetary policy was undoubtedly one factor in the expenditure reductions subsequently approved by the new Government, while over 1995 the Government repeatedly made it clear that one of the pre-conditions of tax cuts in 1996 and 1997 was that these cuts should not necessitate a significant tightening of monetary policy.

The reform of the monetary policy framework was one of the most important elements in the whole reform programme, and it is significant that the legislation which established it was passed by Parliament with the support of Government and Opposition, without a single vote being registered against it.

5. Where to From Here?

THERE IS CLEARLY SCOPE FOR FURTHER REFORM, despite the very substantial progress which has been made over the last 12 years. Government still owns major trading activities which could, in principle, be privatised – New Zealand Post, the Electricity Corporation (and its progeny, Contact Energy), and the Accident Rehabilitation Compensation and Insurance Corporation (ACC), to name just three. Labour market legislation, while substantially more conducive to employment creation than that in many other countries, nevertheless leaves an activist Employment Court reaching decisions which can hardly fail to discourage employers from hiring new staff. In 1994, the provisions of the Minimum Wage Act 1991 were extended to young people. The Employment Contracts Act does not permit employers and employees to opt for at-will employment contracts. We continue to operate in the conviction that monopoly exporters of dairy products, apples and kiwifruit give farmers and growers better returns than competitive exporters. There are some disturbing patterns emerging in the way in which some local authorities are using the provisions of the Resource Management Act (environmental protection legislation). And there can be little doubt that further reform in the areas of income support, education and health-care would yield considerable benefits – personal, social, fiscal and economic.

But what is the likelihood of further reform? Does New Zealand have what Hayek would have called a 'constitution of liberty'? In other words, do the recent reforms amount to a new settlement governing the boundaries between state and society, one that maximises individual freedom under the law? Or could they quite quickly be reversed?

It is not appropriate for me to provide a detailed commentary on the New Zealand political scene, or the platforms of individual parties. But allow me some non-partisan observations.

Public Support for Reforms

First, I believe it is encouraging that there is little public enthusiasm for reversing many of the reforms of the past decade: farmers do not want to return to subsidies; manufacturers do not want to return to high protection; travellers do not want to return to a single monopoly airline; shoppers do not want to go back to restricted shopping hours; nobody wants to go back to six-month waiting lists for a telephone; nobody favours a return to the old government department culture; virtually nobody advocates a return to compulsory unionism; surveys suggest that an overwhelming majority of people are satisfied or very satisfied with their jobs, their job security, and their terms and conditions of employment. There is general support for the Fiscal Responsibility Act, even though there is some disagreement about the details. Even among farmers and manufacturers – those most adversely affected by the last two years of monetary policy tightness – there is no enthusiasm for allowing inflation off the leash, and the overwhelming majority of the members of the present Parliament support not only low inflation but also the framework established by the Reserve Bank Act 1989.

There is much less agreement on some aspects of the tax reforms, or the changes to income support, education and health-care arrangements. While, as already noted, most people do not believe that they themselves have been adversely affected by the Employment Contracts Act, and indeed surveys suggest that most people agree that that Act has been of benefit to the economy, there is quite a widespread view that the legislation was in some way 'unfair', and gave employers an unreasonable advantage vis-à-vis employees. There is quite widespread concern about the extent of foreign investment in New Zealand, with many people worried that foreign ownership of many large institutions and companies represents a 'loss of sovereignty' and a threat to our future prosperity.

Perhaps, after all, Perigo was partly right when he said that New Zealand was 'a country reformed by Hayekians, run by pragmatists and populated by socialists'? My own hunch is that, probably in common with the citizens of other Western countries, New Zealanders accept that socialism does not work in the economy, but remain wedded to the welfare state and a Fabian notion of 'fairness'. The 1995 and 1996 budgets both included quite significant increases in public spending on health and education, and there is no evidence whatsoever that the tax-transfer system has lost any of its legitimacy. New Zealanders still instinctively regard the state as the primary, if not the only, supplier of welfare services of all kinds. It is interesting in this regard that there was considerable public anger at some aspects of the design of the 1996 and 1997 tax cuts: these had been deliberately intended to increase the incentive for those with relatively few skills to seek employment by providing tax reductions for those in employment but few additional advantages to those on benefits. The notion that those on benefits should not get at least the advantage of those in employment was viewed critically by many.

Government Failure to Explain Benefits of Reform

I suspect that current public attitudes also reflect a failure on the part of successive governments and their policy advisers to explain adequately what the benefits of the reform programme are. There has been a failure to explain clearly the benefits for New Zealanders of foreign investment in New Zealand, which has allowed critics to suggest that the open-door policy should be changed so that only foreign investment which benefits New Zealanders should be allowed. There has been a failure to explain the benefits of a less regulated labour market for those who, without that liberalisation, could well have remained unemployed. There has been a failure to explain the benefits of a flatter income-tax scale without tax avoidance opportunities, for economic growth and even for the revenue benefit.[14] There has been a failure

---

[14] Contrary to popular belief, the New Zealand income tax structure remains quite progressive. Under the present tax régime, that is, prior to the tax reductions scheduled to take effect from 1 July 1996, a person with a non-earning spouse and two young children who earns NZ$20,000 pre-tax is liable for a net NZ$777 in income tax (after

to explain the benefit of a more decentralised education system, or of the equity benefits of requiring tertiary students to contribute a modest 25 per cent of their tuition. There has certainly been a failure to explain the benefit – or even the purpose – of the restructured hospital system. There has been a failure to debunk the myth that the reform programme of the last decade has simply further enriched those who were already rich before the reforms began,[15] or the myth that the reform programme has given New Zealand a more unequal income distribution than Australia or the UK. There has been a failure to explain that, at the end of 1984, finance ministers in six OECD countries – New Zealand, Australia, Spain, France, Sweden and the UK – were strong and effective advocates of liberalisation, and all but one of these was a member of a left-of-centre government.[16]

But, lest anybody think that I am blaming others for this failure, there has also been failure in the area for which I myself have major responsibility. It is true that recent market research suggests that some 73 per cent of New Zealanders support low inflation being the Reserve Bank's objective, and 63 per cent believe, despite recent tight monetary policy, that the Bank has been doing a good job in delivering that objective. But I strongly suspect that if asked a slightly different question, a majority of New Zealanders would favour the Bank's using monetary policy also to encourage growth, reduce unemployment, and maintain the exchange rate at a level which helps exporters. My colleagues and I have failed to explain sufficiently convincingly that, while we

---

adjusting for the impact of the Family Support scheme, which is a kind of negative income tax introduced to offset the regressive impact of GST). A person with five times the pre-tax income (NZ$100,000), and the same family circumstances, is liable for income tax of NZ$30,221, almost 39 times the liability of the low-income earner. After the tax reductions scheduled for 1 July 1996 and 1 July 1997, the person earning NZ$20,000 in those family circumstances will actually be in receipt of a net NZ$2,038 from the tax department, while the person earning NZ$100,000 will be paying NZ$27,870 in income tax.

15 Although no wealth statistics exist in New Zealand, it seems very likely that the wealthy New Zealanders of the early 1980s were highly protected manufacturers, owners of large farms, owners of extensive holdings of commercial property, and those lucky enough to have inherited import licences. The reform programme substantially disadvantaged all of those groups.

16 'Economic Reform: New Zealand in an International Perspective', a speech by David Henderson to the Wellington Chamber of Commerce, 28 November 1995.

too strongly support growth, employment and export competitiveness, these are not objectives which monetary policy can actually *deliver*, other than transitorily, and only then at cost to the *long-term* performance of the economy.

Similarly, we have failed to disabuse many New Zealanders of the notion that the framework established by the 1989 Act gives the Bank and its Governor enormous and unfettered power to thwart the will of Parliament, so that critics of the framework can damn it as somehow undemocratic. The reality, of course, is that nothing could be further from the truth: the objective of monetary policy is unambiguously determined by Parliament in the New Zealand framework, and the Governor is held accountable for his performance in achieving that objective. We should have worked harder to make that reality clear.

The best security against the reversal of recent reforms is to continue with reform in order to encourage growth and employment, and to provide increasing opportunities for the unskilled and those on low incomes to raise both their skills and their incomes. Further reform would allow the market order to continue demonstrating its superiority as a generator of wealth and prosperity. At the end of the day, it is actual growth and prosperity, not ideas about the market, that maintain popular support for a free society.

THE IEA HAYEK
MEMORIAL LECTURES

1992   **Privatisation in Eastern Europe**
Professor Jeffrey Sachs, Harvard University

1993   **Two Moral Ideals of Business**
Professor Michael Novak, American Enterprise Institute,
Washington D.C.

1994   **A New Framework for International Economic
Relations**
Dr. Peter D. Sutherland, Director General,
General Agreement on Tariffs and Trade

1995   **State and Society: Restoring the Balance**
Rt. Hon. Francis Maude, Investment banker and
Chairman of the Government's De-regulation Task Force.

1996   **New Zealand's Remarkable Reforms**
Dr. Donald T. Brash, Governor,
Reserve Bank of New Zealand

IEA OCCASIONAL PAPERS

* Wincott Memorial Lectures